Revised Edition

Phillip R. Greaves, 2ND

THE POWER AND VIRTUE OF LUST

FROM THE SEEDS OF DESIRE
SPRINGS THE HARVEST OF LOVE*

---

*   The material in this publication was first presented in the suppressed work, "The Grand Book of the Godless and Free," by the same author.

The Power and Virtue of Lust

2
Amore in a Garden of Bliss

The Power and Virtue of Lust

Amore in a Garden of Bliss

The Power and Virtue of Lust

To Alan: Please forgive me and come back. I just did not recognize you. That is all.

Amore in a Garden of Bliss

It is said that the quickest way to a man's heart is through his stomach. This is not so. Actually, the fastest way to any man's heart is by way of his groin.

The special advantage masturbation grants, to the mindful practitioner, is a position of strength in the pursuit of romantic affairs. Being sexually sufficient within one's self, allows for a more relaxed and confident approach, as opposed to the desperate questing of those who are incomplete.

The Power and Virtue of Lust

Amore in a Garden of Bliss

CLEARLY, THE BEST EXPLANATION for the development of cross-gender, reproductive coupling, is the theory which suggests it evolved from bacterial cannibalization[1]. This theory is based on the fact that certain strains of bacteria will cannibalize, or extract, genetic materials from deceased members of their own strain, in order to repair or improve their genetic code. These bacteria will also exchange genetic elements with living members of their strain for the same purpose.

The connection between this behavior and cross-gender intercourse is indicated by the fact that when egg and sperm unite, among the first things they do are to replicate their own genetic components, exchange parts of their codes, and then continue the process of reproduction.

---

[1] *"Eros And Evolution: A Natural Philosophy Of Sex" by Richard E. Michod*

Amore in a Garden of Bliss

Other Books by
Phillip R. Greaves, 2ND[@]

Society, Reason, Sexuality
(www.createspace.com/3792474) *Our Fountains of Pleasure, Truth, and Order* (www.createspace.com/3617579) *The Power and Virtue of Lust* (www.createspace.com/3624084) *The Grand Delusion* (www.createspace.com/3471913) *A Government of Service to All* (www.createspace.com/3472497) *Water and Oil: Religion and Sex* (www.createspace.com/3672456) *Water and Oil: Sex and Government* (www.createspace.com/3675095) *Water and Oil: Government and Religion* (www.createspace.com/3675108)

[@]   *Titles generally available off and online, in both digital and analog formats*

Amore in a Garden of Bliss

• EXISTENTIAL ENRICHMENT

Although sex has its origin, in the reproductive drive, as the immediate motivation and reward for procreative-coupling, its development as a means for the celebration of life and the most intensely intimate expression of admiration and love began with the advent of subjective consciousness[2] and self-awareness over three thousand years ago[3].

***

The most important question for a being of subjective consciousness is whether life is worth living or not. Consequently, the most important emotional experience is the one which affirms that life is indeed worthwhile.

---

[2]   *A subjective consciousness is an intellect which is self-aware, self-motivated, and self-directed.*
[3]   *"The Origin Of Consciousness In The Breakdown Of The Bicameral Mind" by Julian Jaynes Copyright 1976.*

Amore in a Garden of Bliss

Sex, as both the most intense celebration of life and as the most intimate expression of friendship, admiration, and affection, is the ultimate psycho-physio-emotional affirmation of life's value. As such, sex is the product of the subjective mind's ability to recall the instances and circumstances of genital arousal and orgasmic release and then to consider, project, imagine and pursue these events.

Beyond the psycho-emotional benefits of sex, as the ultimate affirmation of life's value, sex also has many important physiological benefits which are well known. Among these are its ability to relive depression, tension and stress, block minor pain, temporarily alleviate respiratory congestion, promote appetite, improve general health, well-being, and to extend life itself.

Unlike many other values, however, the

life-sustaining and enhancing benefits of sex are readily available to nearly everyone. There are, however, many obstacles to sexual fulfillment -- most of which are unnecessary and easily overcome.

One of the more significant impediments to sexual attainment stems from its connection to procreation. Until recently, cross-gender sexual activity has always carried the risk of producing unwanted offspring. This fact had many negative consequences -- mostly for women and children.

Unintended children were often resented, feared, and mistreated by their unwilling parents. If a child were conceived out-of-wedlock, the pregnancy would sentence the woman to death as a fornicator. *(The child, of course, would die unborn within its mother.)* If the child were conceived in an act of adultery, however, its mother would suffer

11

the same fate only if the child were too noticeably different, in appearance, from its father or siblings.

Often unwanted offspring were killed immediately after being born. Abortions could be induced through dangerous herbal concoctions and beatings -- either of which could result in the woman's death or her permanent sterility. Apart from these harsh realities, pregnancy itself was often a life-threatening condition.

Before the medical benefits of hand washing and the discovery of antibiotics, women frequently died during childbirth or from infection afterwards. For all of these reasons, women had to be especially cautious in their pursuit of erotic enrichment and existential rapture.

There were, of course, other avenues for the pursuit of sexual fulfillment, even before the advent of modern medicine and condoms. Unfortunately, most people were discouraged from pursuing them, or punished if they did. This situation was due entirely to the religions and philosophies which dominated our ancestors through most of our history.

With rare exception, these religions and philosophies viewed sex as little more than a necessary evil and restricted sex to its role as the immediate motivation and reward for coupling. Procreative intercourse, moreover, was confined by these systems of belief to the institution of marriage between a man and a woman or a man and several women. While there were certain advantages to this design, there were many disadvantages as well.

On the plus side, confining erotic pleasure and procreation to the institution of marriage helped to insure a woman would be provided for during her pregnancy and that her offspring would not be immediately orphaned if she died following its birth. Punishing fornication *(sex between unmarried people)*, frequently with execution, served to insure that these safeguards were in place before offspring were conceived.

Executing adulterers helped to protect a man from the hardship of involuntarily providing for children who were not his own. The prohibition against incest *(reproductive sex between closely related persons)*, helped to insure the infusion of fresh, and hopefully better, genes. It also served to prevent the occurrence of genetic defects which often follow after several generations of this practice.

On the minus side, this position leaves little room for love *(a personal value one holds for another)*. Children were often viewed as the property of their parents. As such their

14

parents decided whom they would wed. Parents were, of course, free to choose a partner their child showed affection for.

They were equally free, however, to choose their child's reproductive and/or sexual partner on the basis of genetic considerations, such as health, appearance, or physical strength. Parents might also make their selection with regard to wealth, reputation, religious standing, political position or alliance, traditional affiliations, or friendships among families. A child's parents might also choose, or be obliged, to deny their child both progeny and sexual fulfillment.

A child might be given as an offering to a temple to serve as a celibate priest, priestess or the acolyte of some "god." If a child disagreed with its parents' choice of his wife, her husband, or temple, it was still the child's duty to honor the choice of its parents. This

15

reality, however, often resulted in the child's resentment of its parents, the selected spouse or the temple. This frequently made for bad husbands, wives and a vindictive clergy.

The evolutionary advantage of cross-gender reproduction *(having developed out of bacterial cannibalization)* is inhibited by the institution of marriage -- especially monogamous marriage. In monogamous marriage, the selection for better genes is limited to only one candidate. This greatly slows the rate of genetic improvement among us.

Genetically speaking, it would be better if both men and women were free to continually pursue better genes. Polygamy limits the candidates to either one man or one woman *(women have rarely been allowed this practice)* and several opposite-gender partners.

The disdain these religious philosophies held for sex, moreover, often produced the most damaging psychological effects. Condemning sex as a gross, instinctual act, deprived our ancestors of this most intense celebration of life. It transformed the metaphysical joy of sex into the condemnation of guilt, self-loathing, and shame.

Instead of the affirmation of life's supreme value, the condemnation of sex confirmed a sense of life's curse, a curse of constant misery. Life, in this view, was not a treasure to be cherished, it was a burden and a prison to be endured until the release of death.

These conditions were especially oppressive to women, who were generally considered to be the property of their husbands with no rights, privileges, freedoms or properties of their own. It was considered a woman's lot in life to obey her husband without question and to submit to his every demand -- sexual or otherwise. A man could usually divorce his wife if she displeased him in some way, but a wife could never divorce her husband, not even if he beat or otherwise abused her.

Despite the misery of these circumstances, two groups actually thrived on this situation. Religious leaders and political rulers depended on these dismal conditions for their support, power and wealth. Kings and clergy required a population of duty bound serfs, laborers, subjects and slaves to free them from the necessity of sustaining their lives through their own productive thought and labor.

By limiting sex to its role in procreation, they gained the growing population required to sustain their indolent lives. Also by condemning sexual pleasure as base, these parasites encouraged their victims to view their lot as a duty to be born with resignation and submission. Their condemnation also served to keep the population of their subjects from growing beyond their ability to maintain control.

The dependence of the non-working elite upon the productive working class has always been the true reason behind the elite's condemnation of sex apart from procreative intercourse. It remains the primary motive behind their condemnation of condoms, the birth-control pill, abortion, masturbation, oral sex and homosexuality.

***

In order to impose this code of sexual and reproductive conduct, religious leaders, philosophers, and political authorities alike rely on the common desire for external authorization. To legitimize their authority, they employed a remnant from past ages *(before the development of subjective consciousness)*, when people were directed by auditory and/or or visual hallucinations recognized as "gods." *(Such "gods" are most commonly experienced, in modern times, by those suffering from the mental illness known as schizophrenia.)*

Unlike the hallucinated, earthly "gods" of the past, the "god(s)" of modern times are extra-dimensional and "heard" only by the self-appointed chosen. Such "gods" are imagined rather than hallucinated. They are products of the subjective mind and therefore, inferior to it. All their authority comes from those who believe. They have no independent power or strength.

We, however, are the masters of the

things we imagine. The same priests and philosophers created the myth of an extra-dimensional, heavenly paradise in order to further persuade men to denounce the pleasure and happiness they might otherwise obtain in this world.

The subjective, conscious mind, however, has no need for the hallucinated "gods" of the past, the imaginary "gods" of an indolent elite or the directives of external authorization. All the subjective mind requires, in its quest for meaning and fulfillment, is the exercise of reason through the methods of observation, logical deduction and objective analyses[4].

It is through the guidance of these

---

[4]   *Objectivity is a skill the subjective mind must acquire in order to understand the world within and the cosmos without, in the pursuit of its own prosperity.*

Amore in a Garden of Bliss

means that we have discovered electricity, built skyscrapers, conquered diseases, exploded the atom and liberated sex from the service of procreation.

Our subjective minds work by creating conceptual, analog models of ourselves, our world, our place in it and our relations with others. This allows us to understand, examine and interact, with the world around us, in a way lesser animals can not.

This form of consciousness gives us the ability to retain, conceive, consider, and expand our experience, behavior, identity and ideas in a way which transforms everything we perceive and encounter. It is the very nature of our minds which transforms sex beyond the immediate reward and motivation to reproduce into the embodiment and celebration of life and the most intimate expression of friendship, and affection.

Amore in a Garden of Bliss

The Power and Virtue of Lust

It is our profound need to celebrate the value of life and to experience the most intimate expression of affection, love and admiration which directs and propels our desire for sex, beyond the creation of offspring.

Sex so imbues us with the joy of living, so pervades our being with the emotional confirmation that life is worth living, worth the effort and struggle, that to deny or reject it is to profoundly diminish the value of our existence. To our most intimate and personal associations sex gives a sense of completion which would otherwise go unrealized and unachieved.

Reason affirms that the pursuit and achievement of happiness are essential to our survival and well-being. It is the promise of happiness and the experience of life-sustaining pleasure which motivates both our

Amore in a Garden of Bliss

productive and creative efforts and confirms our conviction that life is indeed worthwhile. The happiest individuals are often the most inventive and artistic.

Sex is a manifestation of happiness, a path to amore in a garden of bliss. As such, sex serves to provide the emotional fuel necessary for the continuous pursuit of life's sustenance. Sex best serves this purpose when indulged regularly apart from the propagation of children.

***

With the invention of the condom, in the eighteenth century, it became possible, for the first time, to both intentionally and consistently liberate cross-gender sex from the service of procreation.

Cross-gender couplings began to enjoy greater reproductive control and freer sexual involvement. The condom also proved effec-

24

tive at inhibiting the transmission of many opportunistic venereal diseases. The later development of the female birth-control pill further liberated sexual engagements between women and men.

Neither the condom nor the pill, however, has proved a hundred percent effective in the liberation of sex or the achievement of conscious reproductive control. Either may fail resulting in unwanted pregnancies. Only permanent, reproductive sterilization completely eliminates the risk of undesired pregnancy resulting from cross-gender sexual involvement.

***

Although certain herbal concoctions were available for both men and women *(before our age of modern medicine)*, the most common method of permanent, procreative sterilization was castration *(the removal of a man's*

25

testicles and sometimes penis).

Understandably, very few volunteered for this procedure. It was usually imposed as a punishment, or as a means of controlling the slave population. *(The Catholic Church once employed castration to preserve the youthful pitch of certain male vocalists.)*

Castration generally put an end to a man's sexual interest as well as his ability to breed. Our modern age of medicine, thankfully, provides us with methods of surgical sterilization which are far less drastic, available to both genders and which permit normal sexual function and appetite. These procedures are well suited for those who choose permanent sterilization.

Sterilization can be a responsible choice for those who suffer from serious genetic deformities or disease. Their parental aspirations should find more productive

26

fulfillment though the adoption of the genetically sound progeny of others. Those who choose to remain reproductively viable must rely on other agencies for sexual fulfillment and reproductive control.

The most universally available avenue for sexual fulfillment and gratification is also the safest and least complicated. It is every bit as free from the risk of unwanted pregnancy as reproductive sterilization, and is equal to celibacy for avoiding the risk of venereal diseases.

***

Masturbation, as the sexual opportunity most readily available to everyone, can deliver practically every benefit sex has to offer. *(Even infants are disposed to engage in this activity until they are repeatedly discouraged from it.)* It is also, unfortunately, the most underrated sexual practice of all.

The Power and Virtue of Lust

The practice of autonomous sexuality is common to most mammalian species as the primary means of relieving frustrated reproductive urgings, or of discharging excessive accumulations of semen. This practice is most frequently indulged among primate species *(especially monkeys, chimpanzees and men)*.

Animal masturbation should not be confused with genital grooming *(cleaning)*, nor can it properly be viewed as sexual in the human sense of the word *(such comparisons are inaccurate and demeaning of our human activity)*. Erotic masturbation is a uniquely human practice in the service of our existential celebration.

Our practice of masturbation is sexual in the sense that it provides a sensual means for the emotional celebration of life and an intensely intimate expression of self-love and esteem. Its unique benefit, however, is that it does so apart from the appraisal, permission or approval of others[5]. Masturbation is self-serve. As such, the quality of the experience it provides is a reflection of self-appraisal. At its best, auto-sexual-stimulation is a self-reliant declaration of self-worth and sufficiency.

Despite its many benefits and near-zero risk factor, solo-sexual gratification *(mastur-bation)* has never received the recognition and praise it so thoroughly deserves. This is partly due to a rather negative attitude commonly held toward this practice.

Many mistakenly view the practice of auto-sexual gratification as an admission of defeat in the pursuit of intimate relations.

---

[5] *Masturbation can give one the power to stop a partner, or spouse, from using sex for control and manipulation.*

Amore in a Garden of Bliss

Such individuals are unable to fully enjoy or achieve the benefits of sexual self-involvement.

Because they view it only as a means to quickly alleviate their frustration, they fail to approach masturbation as a sexual experience. They focus all their attention and effort on their primary reproductive center *(ignoring the rest of their body)* to obtain the most rapid release.

The results of this approach are generally tinged with a deep sense of disappointment, an aftertaste of despair. A more positive attitude produces more rewarding effects and bestows a special advantage.

All those who view masturbation as an autonomous approach to self-gratification, revel in the full bounty of the experience it provides. They stimulate and employ the sensations of their entire body and being in their solitary approach to sexual ecstasy and orgasmic release.

Mind, nipples, skin and anus may join genitalia as centers of sexual excitement and arousal. *(A variety of sexual aids may also be employed.)* Not until the moment of climax do the genitals command the sum of their attention.

Climax explodes with the euphoria of existential rapture and lingers in an aftermath of profound contentment. This, at least, is the soul-enriching experience of those who embrace masturbation as a self-sufficient means to sexual attainment[6].

---

[6]   *I herein declare January 13th (my birthday) World Masturbation Day, and encourage everyone to make a special effort to pleasure themselves on this particular day.*

The Power and Virtue of Lust

The special advantage masturbation grants, to the mindful practitioner, is a position of strength in the pursuit of romantic affairs. Being sexually sufficient within one's self, allows for a more relaxed and confident approach, as opposed to the desperate questing of those who are incomplete.

Unfortunately, the frustration and despair of the forlorn are not the only obstacles to the guiltless abandon of auto-sexual delight. As with all things sexual, masturbation continues to suffer the slanderous attacks of the sex-hating, indolent elite and their pleasure-damning, prudish

---

Of course this does not mean people should not masturbate all year long as well.

Amore in a Garden of Bliss

adherents.

The despoilers of human pleasure are the forces behind such ridiculous absurdities as the notions of frequent masturbation causing blindness, insanity or hairy palms. *(One dictionary, reflecting such influences, identifies self-abuse as a synonym of masturbation, falsely implying that the practice is somehow harmful.)*

As idiotic as these notions are, they are only mild aspersions compared to the pleasure damner's favorite attack on masturbation. This attack consists of the willful misidentification of masturbation as Onanism. Onanism refers to the Biblical sin of Onan when he dishonestly shirked his duty toward his deceased brother.

The brief account of Onan (Genesis 38, 4-10) centers around a matter of Judaic tradition, custom and law, at a time when

Amore in a Garden of Bliss

these terms were synonymous. If a man died without offspring, after taking a wife, it fell upon his surviving brother to mate with his widow and sire an heir to continue his name. This is the situation which confronted Onan. His brother Er, had died leaving no progeny. It fell upon Onan to sire offspring on his brothers behalf.

Onan, however, had no such intention. He had the right to refuse, but doing so would have resulted in his disgrace (Deuteronomy 25, 5-10). Furthermore, Onan may have desired the opportunity for sexual congress which this custom provided. Onan chose to accept this opportunity, but withheld his seed by spilling it on the ground.

This was the sin of Onan, not any act of auto-sexual gratification. It was because of his dishonest abuse of custom that Onan was slain by his "God," according to Judaic myth[7].

Were masturbation the real issue of this account, then it was most unfair for "God" to kill Onan when thousands before him indulged in the same practice and got off scott-free. Onan was far from history's first masturbator, nor its last.

Once a month, every fertile woman produces one mature ovum, however, each time a man ejaculates he releases about two million sperm, only one of which will fertilize an egg[8]. The other one million, nine hundred,

---

[7] *Alternately, Onan might have had a heart attack during intercourse, and just happened to fall out as he ejaculated. In those days anytime someone died suddenly, people assumed it was the hand of "God" at play.*

[8] *The enormous disparity between the number of sperm issued by land dwelling*

---

animals (including man) and the number of eggs to be fertilized, can be traced all the way back to our most distant, ocean-dwelling ancestors, who spawned beneath the waves in the same manner as modern fish and amphibians. For such animals, the reproductive strategy consists of the female laying a cluster of unfertilized ovum on the ocean floor. The male then swims across the clutch spreading his milt over as many eggs as possible. Under this program, there is a much closer ratio of eggs to sperm than in present day land animals and aquatic mammals. Such eggs become fertilized and develop outside the female's body, just as sperm dose with respect to the male. This allowed the female to produce a great many more offspring than animals whose eggs are fertilized and/or or gestated internally. As evolution carried forward into fish whose eggs were fertilized internally and later into mammals, where fertilization and gestation both occur within the female, evolutionary pressures forced a decrease in the number of eggs produced at one time. For the male,

---

however, there were few, if any, pressures to reduce the number of sperm released, as insemination and gestation continued to occur outside the male's body, and the production of semen continued to be quite inexpensive. This is the cause for the overwhelming difference between the number of eggs produced vs. the number of sperm deployed to fertilize them. On the other hand, if a "supreme being" had engineered all life on earth, "It" would most likely have designed the male reproductive system to release only enough sperm to fertilize the females' eggs and little else.

Amore in a Garden of Bliss

ninety nine thousand, nine hundred and ninety-nine are completely wasted, so it is extremely unlikely that "God" would be concerned over some spilled semen.

Since only one sperm will join with an ovum, this is actually the only sperm that matters. The rest would be wasted by "God's" design anyway *(if such a being truly existed)*.

In their efforts to dominate and control the productive, upon whom they depend, the parasites among us use the story of Onan to condemn masturbation as a sin against the imaginary "God" they have conditioned others to believe in. They accomplish this by preaching that "God" slew Onan for wasting his semen, without any reference to the circumstances of the biblical account.

Through this means, these spiritual tyrants equate auto-sexual gratification with such transgressions as fornication and adultery *(both were punishable by death)*. The purpose behind this distortion is both to reinforce procreative intercourse, as the only acceptable sexual outlet, and to infect autonomous fulfillment with esteem-corroding guilt.

Guilt, in turn, acts to undermine confidence generating self-doubt and a profound sense of inadequacy. These are the prerequisites for the unquestioned acceptance of unfounded assertions claiming arbitrary authority.

A vague reference to an "...uncleanness that chanceth him by night..." (Deuteronomy 23, 10), has been used as a disparagement of masturbation, semen, and sex in general. This passage is commonly believed to refer to a nocturnal emission *(a wet dream)* but, considering the surrounding text, it could just as easily refer to urination *(bed wetting)*, or a bout of diarrhea.

Taking this uncleanness as an involuntary spilling of sperm, however, allowed religious authorities to promote the idea that semen made one spiritually impure. To intentionally risk such pollution, through auto-sexual stimulation, had to be among the bases of sins.

In the Middle-Ages, nocturnal emissions took on an even more sinister interpretation. They were believed to be the result of demonic possessions by succubae *(in the case of male victims)* or incubi *(in the case of women).* This superstitious fear of wet dreams contributed to the vampire legends. *(Interestingly, in Bram Stoker's "Dracula," the vampire is depicted as having hairy palms.)*

• BREAKING THE CHAINS

Fortunately, the machinations of clergy and potentates are losing their influence and power. The misrepresentations and twisting of recorded myths, used to promote their agendas of control are collapsing. Their demise is due, in part, to the achievement of a man named Gutenberg and his defiant stand against the Catholic church. When Johann Gutenberg invented movable type in the fourteenth century, he opened the way to the mass production of books and broke the monopoly the Catholic church held over all learning.

***

Prior to Gutenberg, all books had to be copied by hand. The time and effort it took to reproduce a single copy was enormous. As a result, books were very expensive and owning one was well beyond the means of the average person. The Catholic church alone possessed the resources needed to provide publication. Only the nobility held sufficient wealth for purchase.

Amore in a Garden of Bliss

The Power and Virtue of Lust

The average person could neither read nor write and was actively discouraged from learning. To the authorities of the time, the prospect of an educated populace posed a greater threat than famine or war.

Authorities of church and state depended on the ignorance of the masses and the manipulations of recorded myths, along with the expository teachings of the Bible, to exercise control and demand the submission of their subjects. To secure their authority they had to maintain exclusive control over these writings.

For this reason, the average person was prohibited from owning or even reading the Bible. The authority of the clergy was beyond questioning. The text and meaning of the holy writings were whatever the religious authorities claimed. No one, apart from the church, could prove, or even know, otherwise.

Amore in a Garden of Bliss

The creation of movable type greatly reduced the cost of publication and the expense of book ownership. Gutenberg was willing to sell his publications to anyone who could pay his price. Books became both more affordable and available. The publishing monopoly of the church was broken.

Gutenberg defied the exclusive control the Catholic church held over scripture. He chose the Bible as the first large work to be published with his movable type. The Gutenberg Bible became the first collection of Judaic-Christian scripture available to individuals outside the clergy and ruling class.

As the Bible became accessible to anyone who could read, the misrepresentations of the clergy were exposed. The mindful reader could examine the story of Onan, understand its context and perceive it bore no connection to auto-sexual gratification. Many other distortions were also revealed.

The few who could read began to teach those who wished to learn. Individuals acquired the knowledge and courage to dispute the teaching of the church. New religious sects formed around rival interpretations of scripture. A religious reformation had begun.

At first, this reformation had little affect regarding sexual matters. The Bible does, in fact, contain a harsh reproductive and/or sexual code, prescribing death for a wide range of infractions (Leviticus 20, 10-21). This allowed the clergy to maintain its repressive control over sex, despite the collapse of their scriptural distortions. The new clergies followed the old in condemning sexual pleasure and restricting it to its reproductive role within monogamous marriage.

Jesus had propagated the idea of a thought crime and/or sin when he declared a man guilty of adultery if he even looked at a woman with a lustful eye (Matthew 5, 28). This condemnation was applied, by extension, to masturbation which frequently involves imaginary, sexual imagery. *(Although it is possible, with practice and effort, to masturbate without it.)* If this notion were actually applied in practice, it could subject everyone who purchased or viewed pornographic material to execution for adultery or fornication.

The opportunity to read scripture oneself, however, did more than reveal the machinations of the clergy. It allowed the mindful reader to confront the many inconsistencies, contradictions, bigotries, errors and absurdities within the Bible itself.

45

In time, the more courageous began to question not only the authority of the church, but also that of the scriptures and even the existence of "God." Everything became subject to re-examination through the application of reason to experience and observation. Sexual attitudes became subject to change.

Over five hundred years have passed since the invention of movable type, the Gutenberg Bible and the beginning of the religious reformation. The sexual tyranny of the pretentious, power-seeking elite, however, continues to afflict us.

Within this decade (the 1990s) the Surgeon General of an allegedly free country *(the United States of America)* was removed from her office for broaching the subject of masturbation before an audience of Catholic, Islamic and Judaic clergy, regarding the problem of over population. The name of this outspoken, progressive woman was Joycelyn Elders.

Despite this and other setbacks, the revolution continues and succeeds. Reason and knowledge persist in dispelling the darkness of ignorance, superstition and oppression.

Psychologists and medical experts agree that auto-sexual gratification is both wholesome and normal. Masturbation even provides monogamous couples with a means to compensate for differences in sexual appetite.

It also serves as a responsible outlet for individuals afflicted with serious genetic deformities or disease, those who suffer from incurable sexual infections and those whose sexual inclinations might place their lives and liberty at risk within an intolerant society.

Masturbation is not, however, always synonymous with auto-sexual gratification.

Reciprocal masturbation and mutual fondling can play an important role in sexual foreplay for couples. They also provide couples and groups with the opportunity to share and explore sexual pleasures and practices apart from reproductive intercourse and the risk of pregnancy.

• A WORLD OF INDULGENCE

There is yet another opportunity for sexual fulfillment, and existential celebration, which is also as free from the risk of unintended pregnancy as are sexual abstinence, reproductive sterilization and auto-sexual gratification.

***

Unlike sexual abstinence and auto-sexual delight, however, it provides an avenue for the most intimate expression of friendship, desire and love. This dimension of sexual attainment is the practice of monogender, or unigender, sexual congress.

When individuals of the same gender engage in sexual relations, the possibility of producing offspring is nonexistent. This, however, is far from the only benefit to be derived from such relations.

Single-gender sex provides an opportunity for the sexual appreciation and empathetic understanding of one's own gender which is unavailable through any other means. No male can understand or accurately empathize with the gender specific, emotional experiences or sensations of a woman.

He can, however, fully identify with the gender specific sensations of another man. Moreover, the same is true of women in regard to their relations with others. For this reason monogender sex represents the ultimate consummation of same gender bonding[9].

Single-gender, unigender and mono-gender are all just creative ways of saying homosexual, but that is the topic at hand. If

---

[9]   *Many heterosexuals are so hetero-centric that they simply must impose their own sexual dynamics onto everyone else. So, because a heterosexual couple is made up of a man and a woman, every other form of sexuality must conform to the hetero pattern in some respect. Therefore, heterosexuals often insist that homosexual couples must contain a man and a female-substitute-male, or a women and a male-substitute-female. The idea that two men can enjoy each other sexually, as men, or that two women can enjoy one another, as women, is so foreign to many heterosexuals as to be beyond their conception. Unfortunately, many homosexuals buy-in to this nonsense and adopt this stereotype, which comes not from homosexuality, but from a reproductive imperative.*

Amore in a Garden of Bliss

the world were mostly gay, what might the benefits be?

For one, the rate of population growth would slow quite a bit. Also the value and care of children would increase and improve (*due to the greater cost of parenthood*). Since homosexuals can not reproduce with their partners, they must go outside of their relations to find a member(s) of the opposite sex to have (a) child(ren) in the traditional way, or opt for artificial insemination.

Within such a system, those seeking children would be much more likely to have some actual money to care for (a) child(ren). It is also likely that more people would adopt under such circumstances.

The practice of homosexuality could actually improve our species, by encouraging the selection of surrogates and donors according to genetic considerations and aesthetic values, while allowing sexual indulgence without issue. Furthermore, within such a social order, individuals would always be free to shop for the best genetic material, per child they chose to create. Moreover, the practice of gay sex is open to everyone, despite some opinions to the contrary.

Because same-gender-sex never produces offspring, the taboos regulating procreation are pointless and without meaning, inside a homosexual context, and can be safely ignored. Therefore, if a father has mutually consenting sex with his grown son there is no harm done and no reason for either to be ashamed[10].

---

[10]   *Unless either of them is breaking his vows to another, such as to a wife or husband, of promised fidelity.*

Amore in a Garden of Bliss

The same is true of homosexual relations between freely consenting brothers, same-gender-cousins[11], uncles and their adult nephews, even grandfathers and their grown grandsons. As long as everyone feels comfortable and uncoerced, in such relations, there is no reason to feel ashamed in them. The same reality exists with regard to sexual relations among women toward each other.

Several surveys and studies show, that when either of two identical twins is gay, fifty-one percent of the time, the other twin is gay too. This information is commonly used to claim that homosexuality is genetic. If this were true, however, a percentage much closer to a hundred should be expected.

---

[11] *This section is about adult on adult relations only, including freely consenting brothers and same-gender-cousins.*

The Power and Virtue of Lust

The "it is genetic" crowd is just trying to avoid responsibility for the way they are, but no excuse is needed. Homosexual practices, and romantic involvements, have much to offer and can be of benefit to both individuals and societies. So, join the party, if you will.

• LOVER WANTED

My ideal man is no older than thirty-five and no younger than eighteen. He has straight, black hair and medium brown skin. He is no taller than six foot and is of aboriginal-American, Asian, or Mexican decent.

My ideal guy is intelligent without being condescending. He is trim and lean. Ideally, he should be uncut with a smooth body and a boyish face. At best, he should be versatile, sexually, but I can wait a little for him to become so.

This is my ideal, but I may consider others depending on how close they are to what I have described here. As for myself, I'm white and a little overweight, but I'm working on that. I have my own home and a great car, for anyone who cares about such things. Interested parties should email me at:

RayGreaves2@yahoo.com